Disney · PIXAR

FINDING DORY

MEMORY GAMES
AND BRAIN TEASERS

EDDA USA

**FINDING DORY
MEMORY GAMES & BRAIN TEASERS**
© 2016 Disney/Pixar

Author: Olafur Gunnar Gudlaugsson
Layout and design: Olafur Gunnar Gudlaugsson
Cover design: Olafur Gunnar Gudlaugsson
Printing: Printed in Canada

Distributed by Midpoint Book Sales & Distribution

ISBN: 9781940787411

www.eddausa.com

WELCOME

DO YOU LIKE MEMORY GAMES AND BRAIN TEASERS?
SURE YOU DO. OTHERWISE YOU WOULD'NT BE
HOLDING THIS BOOK!

THIS BOOK IS FULL OF FUN GAMES THAT WILL TEST
YOUR VAST ABILITIES. CHALLENGING ANAGRAMS AND
GREAT REBUS PUZZLES. INGENIOUS MATCHSTICK
PUZZLES, PICTURE WORDS AND MORE!

DIVE INTO THE OCEAN WITH DORY AND FRIENDS AND
START PLAYING!

KEEP ON SWIMMING !

OBSERVE & REMEMBER

AS WE ALL KNOW, DORY IS AFFLICTED WITH SHORT-TERM MEMORY LOSS. THIS FUN GAME CAN HELP TRAIN THE BRAIN'S ABILITY TO REMEMBER WITH OBSERVATION AND RECOLLECTION.

1 In a closed room, arrange various objects on a table. They can be of different sizes, shapes and color. Make sure you have enough space between the objects so they can be easily identified. The amount of objects is variable, but let's start with 10 objects.

2 Cover the objects with something dark and call in a contestant. Note: For this game you can have as many contestants as you want, but allow for the time factor.

3 The contestant stands in front of the table and is instructed to remember all the things he/she sees on the table. The cover is removed.

4 The contestant has 15 seconds to observe and remember.

5 Place the cover over the objects.

6 Allow 1 minute to pass and ask the contestant to list as many objects as possible from the table.

7 The contestant with the most remembered objects wins.

8 If there are two or more contestants with the same amount remembered, change the items and add 5 more.

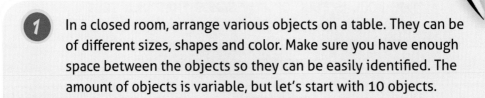

AQUATIC BRAIN BOOSTERS 1

HERE ARE SOME GREAT RIDDLES TO HELP YOU TRAIN THAT BEAUTIFUL BRAIN OF YOURS!

1

QUESTION:
I can bring tears to your eyes, make you smile, and reverse time. I form in an instant but I last a life time.
What am I?

2

QUESTION:
Almost everyone needs it, asks for it, gives it, but almost nobody takes it.
What is it?

3

QUESTION:
A whalrus and a young one were swimming. The young one was the whalrus' son, but the whalrus was not the young ones father.
Who was the whalrus?

4

QUESTION:
If two's company and three's a crowd, what are four and five?

MEMORY EXTRACTION

TO HELP DORY TRAIN HER BRAIN WHY NOT TRY THE CLASSIC MEMORY GAME. YOU CAN TRAIN BY YOURSELF OR PLAY WITH ANOTHER. EITHER WAY IT'S A GREAT MEMORY EXTRACTION METHOD.

1 Scan and print out 2 pages of Dory and friends on the opposite page. You should have 2 of each type, 24 in all.

2 Use a black marker to thoroughly cover the opposite sides of the characters.

3 Scramble the cards and arrange them upside down on a table in a 6x4 grid.

4 Take turns selecting and turning over any two cards at a time. If you have a match, keep them. If not, turn them back over.

5 Try to remember what each character looks like and where it is located.

6 Once all the characters have been matched, the player with the most pairs wins.

HOW MANY MAMMALS?

THE DIFFERENCE BETWEEN A MAMMAL AND A FISH CAN BE CONFUSING, ESPECIALLY IF BOTH CAN LIVE UNDER WATER! CAN YOU IDENTIFY THE MAMMALS IN THIS PICTURE?

WHAT'S NOT RIGHT?

WHICH PICTURE DOES NOT BELONG HERE?

WHO'S THIS?

A QUESTION OF DIFFERENCE

THE VAST OCEANS OF THE WORLD ARE FILLED WITH COUNTLESS DIFFERENT SPECIES OF FISH AND OTHER AQUATIC LIFEFORMS. HOW MANY FISH SPECIES CAN YOU SEE IN THIS PICTURE? HERE'S A TIP: SIZE AND COLOR DON'T MATTER.

THE PUZZLING WORD

MIX TOGETHER THE INITIALS OF RHENIUM FROM THE PERIODIC TABLE WITH AN INDIVIDUAL THAT BELONGS TO A CLUB. WHAT WORD DO YOU GET?

AN OBVIOUS ANSWER?

WHY ARE SOME LETTERS ABOVE OR UNDER THE SEA LEVEL?

A E F H I K L M N T V W X Y Z

B C D G J O P Q R S U

AQUANAGRAM

GENIES WIMP MONK

WEEPING INKS MOM

KNEEING SWIM MOP

ALL THESE SENTANCES CAN BE REARRANGED INTO THE SAME SENTENCE. WHAT IS IT?

HOT & COLD

YOU WILL NEED YOUR WHITS ABOUT YOU
IN THIS SUPER-FUN GAME!

1 A player leaves the room, while the others select something for him to do, such as offering Bill a glass of milk, or standing on a chair and opening the center window from the top.

2 The player is not permitted to ask questions.

3 When the player is anywhere in the room except the right place, the others say, "You're cold."

4 When the player approaches Bill or the center window, as the case may be, they say, "You're getting warm," "You're getting warmer," "You're getting hot."

5 When the player is close to the precise object, they say "You're hot."

6 When the player actually does it, they say, "You're sizzling—that's it!"

TOUCH AND FEEL !

HONE YOUR DEDUCTION ABILITIES WITH THIS INGENIOUS GAME OF TOUCH AND FEEL!

Take three boxes, and put three different items in each. Ask the players to put their hand in the box and guess what these items are and which belong to the sea. Suggestions; a sea shell; wet cotton wool; a wet shoelace; a cochlea, etc.

TURN MARLIN AROUND !

MOVE THREE STICKS AND MAKE MARLIN SWIM IN THE OPPOSITE DIRECTION.

WHAT IS IT?

THIS CLASSIC BRAIN-GAME OF 20 QUESTIONS NEVER GOES OUT OF STYLE!

1 One player writes down the name of an object anywhere in the world. The slip is folded and placed in sight of all.

2 The other players ask twenty questions, in rotation, and must guess the object by the time the twentieth question has been answered.

3 Questions must be answered with YES, NO or I DON'T KNOW.

4 The player naming the object selects the one to be questioned next.

5 A typical game, with the Great Barrier Reef as the object, might proceed like this:

Q. Is it in existence now? A. Yes.

Q. Does it belong to the animal kingdom? A. No.

Q. Is it used by any members of the animal kingdom? A. Yes

Q. Is it used by men? A. No.

Q. Is it something to eat? A. No.

Q. Is it something to wear? A. No.

Q. Is it a means of transportation? A. No.

Q. Is it a public building? A. No.

Q. Is it in the sea? A. Yes.

Q. Is it part of the ground? A. Yes.

Q. Is it alive? A. Yes.

Q. Is it in the Pacific Ocean? A. Yes.

Q. Is it in the movie Finding Dory? A. Yes.

Q. Is it the Great Barrier Reef? A. Yes.

WHAT'S WITH THE REBUS?

YOU MAY BE FLUENT IN WHALE-SPEAK BUT CAN YOU UNDERSTAND THESE PHRASES?

**FUNNY FUNNY
WORDS WORDS
WORDS WORDS**

MILONELION

I'M **YOU**

**GIVE GET
GIVE GET
GIVE GET
GIVE GET**

AN OBVIOUS ANSWER?

MOST FISH USUALLY BREED MANY, MANY LITTLE FISH.

PHILLIP CAME FROM A RATHER SMALL HATCH. HIS MOTHER, SHELLY, ONLY HAD FOUR CHILDREN. THREE WERE NAMED NANA, NENE, AND NINI.

SO WHAT IS THE FOURTH CHILD'S NAME?

SEAFACTS

BLUE TANG

Dory is a Blue Tang or Palette Surgeonfish. These fish are only blue when they reach adulthood. They live in coral reefs in the tropical Indo-Pacific area and usually hide among coral branches when they're alarmed. Blue Tangs eat zooplankton.

END

START

HELP DORY FIND HER WAY HOME

AQUATIC BRAIN BOOSTERS 2

MORE GREAT RIDDLES FOR BRAIN TRAINING!

1

QUESTION:
Which word in the dictionary is spelled like non-vertibrae?

2

QUESTION:
Which word becomes shorter when you add two letters to it?

3

QUESTION:
What comes once in a minute, once in a moment and once in a thousand years?

4

QUESTION:
If you take away the whole, some will still remain. What is it?

5

QUESTION:
You are swimming in a race, and you swim past the person in second place. What place are you in?

QUICK REACTIONS

THE IMPORTANCE OF FAST REFLEXES IS OFTEN UNDERESTIMATED, AS THIS CRAZY GAME WILL TEACH YOU!

1 All the players, except one, sit in a circle. There is one vacated spot for the player left out.

2 The player left out, let's call him the Namer, walks around the outside of the circle, tapping on the head of each child as they pass them, and with each tap, calling out the name DORY.

3 After a while, and without warning, the Namer changes the name Dory into NEMO, and starts running round the circle to get back round to the vacated spot.

4 The player called NEMO has to get up as quickly as possible and try and catch the Namer.

5 If the Namer can get back round the circle before being caught, they sit down, and NEMO does the walking around.

6 If not, the same Namer has to go again.

WHAT'S WITH DORY?

ONLY ONE PICTURE OF DORY IS THE CORRECT ONE.

AQUANAGRAMS

SCOOTS UP

HARKS

LA HEW

TREPANS

RYE MOM

WHAT DO THESE ANAGRAMS MEAN?
HINT: THEY ARE ALL ONE WORDS.

CLOWNFISH

Marlin and Nemo are ane-monefish, or more popularly, clownfish. They are native to the warmer waters of the Indian and Pacific oceans, including the Great Barrier Reef and the Red Sea. Clownfish are omnivorous, which means they can eat anything!

THE NAME GAME

THIS NIFTY GAME HELPS US TRAIN THE BRAIN AND SHARPEN OUR SHORT TERM MEMORY FUNCTIONS! SOMETHING DORY WOULD WELL APPRECIATE!

1 All the players sit in a circle.

2 One random player starts the game by saying a name. This can be a first or last name, but it has to be a proper name, so everyone remembers it.

3 The player to the left says the same name and adds another name that starts with the last letter of the first name.

4 The third player then says the first two names and adds a third name that starts with the last letter of the second name.

5 This goes on and on until the chain is broken when one player can´t remember the sequence of names.
The group then starts over with a new name.

6 **Variations on the game:**
1. The players can, of course, say the names in funny voices, even in whale-speak!
2. When a player is having difficulty remembering the name-sequence, other players may help.
3. Try choosing names of famous people or characters

JOHN-NEMO-OSCAR
RUBERT-TOMAS-SUSAN
NITZE-EMMY-YURI-IRINA
ALBERT-TIM-MARLIN ...

CLOSE UP CHARACTERS

IDENTIFY THE CHARACTERS IN THESE PICTURES

BREAK THE CODE !

DECIPHER THIS IMPORTANT MESSAGE!

WHAT IS THE RULE?

THERE ARE ALWAYS THINGS IN OUR LIVES AND ENVIRONMENT THAT ARE CONSTANT. ONE COULD SAY THAT THEY ARE THE RULES. LET'S EXPLORE THIS CONCEPT FURTHER WITH THIS EXELENT GAME.

1 Gather 5-10 players. One player is chosen to start the game. He/she is called the rulemaker.

2 The rulemaker decides what the rule is. This can be anything. For instance, the rulemaker says: "When I go into the sea, I can take a **tomato** with me." Here he decides that **red, round vegetables are the rule**.

3 The next player then says: "When I go into the sea, I can take **broccoli** with me," thinking the rule is only **vegetables**.
The rulemaker replies: "No, you can't take broccoli into the sea."

4 Another player says: "When I go into the sea, I can take a **chili pepper** with me," thinking the rule is only **red vegetables**.
The rulemaker replies: "No, you can't take a chili pepper into the sea."

5 This can go on for some time until a player finally says:
"When I go into the sea, I can take a **red bell pepper** with me."
The rulemaker replies: "Yes, you can take a red bell pepper into the sea. Do you know why?"
Then that player may guess what the rule is. If he gets it right the game is over and he can make the next rule. If not he is out and the game continues.

A DIFFERENT DESTINY

HOW MANY DIFFERENT DESTINY'S ARE THERE?

LAND OR SEA?

GROUP THE WORDS
WITH THEIR OPPOSITES

SWIM DRY TREES
COLD TIGER
WALK MAMMAL
WATER HOT
ELEPHANT WHALE
WET AIR SHARK
KELP FISH

BELUGA WHALE

Bailey is a Beluga Whale, often called melonhead, beluga or sea canary, due to its high-pitched twitter. They live in the Arctic oceans around the North Pole. These sea mammals form large groups and can live up to 70-80 years. They live on all kinds of smaller fish and other sea life.

ANSWER NOW!

1 Prepare in advance 9 extremely easy questions with only yes and no answers.

Example: Q: Does 2 plus 2 equal 4?
Q: Is grass geen?
Q: Is water dry?
Q: Can an octopus fly?

Include one difficult question that needs a long answer.
The players do not need to know the answer.
Example: Q: Why is the sky blue?
Put that question in the middle of the list of questions.

2 Each player is called, one at a time, into a secluded room.

3 The player is informed that he will be bombarded with quick questions, and that he must answer them within 2 seconds. He is also informed that all the answers need not be correct.

4 Ask the questions quickly and right after the given answers. Give the players no time to think.

5 If a player hesitates for more than 2 seconds he is out of the game. The players with the most correct answers win.

NOTE: Usually players will hesitate on the difficult question. The trick here is to answer with "Pass" or "I don´t know" .

GEOMETRIC QUIZ

YOU HAVE FIVE FISH IN A POND AND EACH FISH SLAPS
FINS WITH EVERY OTHER FISH EXACTLY ONCE. HOW MANY
TOTAL FINSLAPS HAPPEN?

AN OBVIOUS ANSWER?

UNDER THE OCEAN YOU CANNOT TAKE A PICTURE
OF A DARK BLUE FISH WITH A YELLOW FIN.
WHY NOT?

AQUANAGRAMS

CEREAL FOR PHIS RIVED

AURA QI MU

BEAM RUINS

CANOE

WHAT DO THESE ANAGRAMS MEAN?
HINT: THEY ARE ALL ONE WORDS.

LET'S TELL A STORY

GET THOSE CREATIVE JUICES FLOWING AND IMPROVISE!

3-7 players sit in a circle. One player starts a story with a sentence and the next follows up on that sentence, continuing the story. This game normally ends with the players writhing on the floor, laughing uncontrollably.

SO, THIS FISH SWIMS INTO THE KELP-FORREST ...

... AND FINDS A BEAUTIFUL MERMAID ...

... WHO TELLS HIM THAT HE SHOULD GO BACK HOME ...

... BECAUSE HE FORGOT TO LOCK THE DOOR TO HIS HOUSE ...

... REALLY?!

... NO, I WAS JUST ... NEVER MIND.

THE EYES HAVE IT !

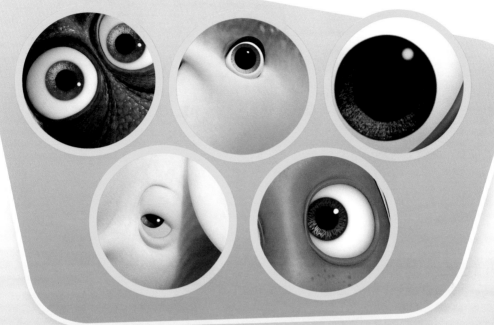

IDENTIFY THE CHARACTERS IN THESE PICTURES

WHAT IS THIS?

S + 🧍 ←

DORY SAYS

THERE IS A HUGE DIFFERENCE BETWEEN WHAT YOU SEE AND WHAT YOU HEAR.

1 4 or more players gather in a room or outside.

2 One random player is designated as Dory and is in control of the game.

3 All the other players must obey Dory and do what Dory tels them to do. BUT players must ONLY obey if Dory begins the sentence with: "DORY SAYS ..." before issuing the instructions.

4 **Examples:**
DORY: "Dory says jump on one leg."
Everyone jumps on one leg.
DORY: "Dory says jump on both legs."
Everyone jumps on both legs.

5 Dory can fool the players by not saying "DORY SAYS ..." before the instructions. Those who get fooled are out of the game.

6 Another trick to fool the players is for Dory just to do something, without saying anything. Those who get fooled are also out of the game.

7 The one player that is left gets to be Dory in the next round.

AQUATIC BRAIN BOOSTERS 3

MORE FUN RIDDLES FOR THAT BEAUTIFUL BRAIN

1

QUESTION:
How far can a fish swim into a coral reef?

2

QUESTION:
You can swallow it, but it can also swallow you. What is it?

3

QUESTION:
Imagine you're in a room with no windows or doors. In the room is a hungry shark who wants to eat you. How do you get out?

4

QUESTION:
In what month do fish sleep the least?

5

QUESTION:
There is an abandoned aquarium in an empty house. The aquarium has three large fish and three small fish. But after a week, one large fish and two small fish die. How many remain in the aquarium?

THE HARBORMASTER

YOU WILL NEED ALL YOUR FOCUSING ABILITIES IN THIS CLASSIC QUESTION AND ANSWER GAME.

1 2 players face each other. One asks the questions the other answers them.

2 In this game the one who is asking wants to know what you did with all the kelp the Harbormaster gave you.

3 There are four words the player answering must never use: No, yes, black and white. If any of those words are used in the answer the player loses.

4 Example:
Q: What did you do with all the kelp the Harbormaster gave you?
A: I sold it.
Q: Sold it?
A: Absolutely!
Q: Did you buy anything for the money?
A: I bought a car.
Q: A white car?
A. No, a blue car .... argh!

5 The player lost the game because he used the word no.

LET'S FREE NEMO !

MOVE 2 STICKS TO CREATE 2 SQUARES AND 5 RECTANGLES, AND FREE NEMO IN THE PROCESS. ALL THE STICKS MUST BE FLAT ON THE SURFACE.

WHAT IS THE LAW?

YOU ARE IN THE ARCHIPELAGO AND THERE IS ONLY ONE LAW. THERE ARE ALL KINDS OF FISH, BUT NO TUNA. THERE ARE SHARKS BUT NO WHALES. YOU CAN BE FAMISHED, BUT NEVER HUNGRY. AND YOU CAN BE CRUSHED BUT NOT BROKEN. WHAT IS THE LAW?

WHALE SHARK

Destiny is a whale shark, the largest fish in the world! It's a fish like a shark, but it eats like a whale. The whale shark lives in all tropical and warm-temperate seas. The largest confirmed whale shark had a length of 41.50 ft and some unconfirmed sightings tell of a much larger specimen. Wow!

FIND THE LEADER

OBSERVE, DETECT, DEDUCE AND FINALLY ACCUSE!

1 Players from 5 to 25 gather in a room or outside.

2 One player is chosen to find the leader and is sent away for the time being.

3 Meanwhile, the other players decide who will be the leader and the secluded player is then asked to come back.

4 The leader moves in a way that all the other players can mimic; touch his ear, cross his arms or something. The main thing is to be as inconspicuous as possible.

5 The other players may block the view of the seeker by forming a ring around him, but may not hinder him from moving.

6 If the seaker thinks he has found the leader he shouts: "I accuse!" and points to the player he suspects. If he is wrong the game continues.

7 When the leader is found he is sent away and must search for the leader in the next round.

IMPORTANT MESSAGE

YOU ARE FABULOUS, JUST THE WAY YOU ARE

AN OBVIOUS ANSWER?

NO SOONER SPOKEN THAN BROKEN.
WHAT IS IT?

WHAT'S GOING TO HAPPEN?

+ LL

TRUE OR FALSE

IT'S TIME TO FIND OUT HOW WELL YOU REALLY KNOW YOUR FAMILY AND FRIENDS

1 Players range from 2 to 15 or more and you will need paper and pencils.

2 Each player writes down three facts about themselves, two true and one false.

3 The true facts cannot be too obvious and the false fact has to be very credible.

4 The players gather in a circle and one player starts reading aloud his "facts", without revealing the true nature of what is true or false.

5 The group then discusses these facts and tries to detect which fact is true or false. They finally come to an agreement and the player reveals what is true or false.

6 The next player reads his "facts".

7 When the game is over you will be wiser about your family and/or friends.

I'M A WHALE
I'M A SHARK
I LOVE KNITTING

PALINDROMES

THESE WONDERFUL WORDS HAVE THE UNIQUE ABILITY OF BEING THE SAME WHEN READ FROM BOTH SIDES! HERE ARE A FEW RIDDLES WITH PALINDROMES FOR ANSWERS.

EXAMPLES: CIVIC, HANNAH, EVE HE DID, EH?

WHICH CALL FOR HELP WHEN WRITTEN IN CAPITAL LETTERS IS THE SAME FORWARDS, BACKWARDS AND UPSIDE DOWN?

WHAT SAILS ON THE OCEAN AND ONLY HAS ONE ROWER?

YOU AND I HAVE A PAIR.
I HAVE SAID IT TWICE.

THE FAMOUS POP BAND FROM SWEDEN

WHAT AM I?

WHAT IS THE BEGINNING OF ETERNITY, THE END OF TIME AND SPACE; THE BEGINNING OF EVERY END AND THE END OF EVERY PLACE?

THE RHYME GAME

BEING SILLY HELPS LOSEN THE BRAIN, AND THIS GREAT VARIATION ON THE NAME GAME IS JUST PLAIN FUN AND SILLY.

1 All the players sit in a circle.

2 One random player starts the game by saying a word. This can be any word, but it has to be a proper word, so everyone remembers it.

3 The player to the left says the same word and adds another word that rhymes with the first.

4 The third player then says the first two words and adds a third word that rhymes with the former two.

5 This goes on and on until the chain is broken when one player can´t remember the sequence of words or can't add to the rhyme. The group then starts over with a new word.

Variations on the game:
The players can, of course, say the words in funny voices, even in whale-speak!

FISH-DISH-WISH-SWISH
DORY-CORY-LORY-SORRY
HAM-JAM-BAM
STRING-BLING-FLING-BRING

LET'S FREE NEMO ... AGAIN!

NEMO IS CAUGHT AGAIN! MOVE THREE STICKS TO CREATE THREE EQUAL SQUARES AND FREE NEMO IN THE PROCESS

AQUANAGRAMS

CAR ON

PORE

SO LIAR

PANIC AT

WHAT DO THESE ANAGRAMS MEAN?
HINT: THEY ARE ALL ONE WORDS.

WHAT AM I?

ALIVE WITHOUT BREATH,

AS COLD AS DEATH,

NEVER THIRSTY,

EVER DRINKING,

WHEN TIRED,

NEVER WINKING.

WHO IS IT?

OUR ABILITY TO GATHER INFORMATION THROUGH TOUCH AND FEEL IS IMPORTANT, ESPECIALLY WHEN DEPRIVED OF ONE OF YOUR MAJOR SENSES.

1 Players can range from 5 to 10. One player is chosen and blindfolded. He/she is called Touchy.

2 5 other players form a random row and Touchy is led in front of them.

3 The object of the game is for Touchy to recognize as many players as possible within a 3 minute timeframe.

4 Touchy may touch the faces of the players but nothing else. Touchy may also ask one question from the player he is touching, but not about the identity of the player. That player may answer in a weird voice or a whisper.

5 If some of the players are very tall, have them squat down to the approximate size of the other players.

6 If Touchy thinks he has discovered the identity of a player he can just say his name and carry onto the next player. Once the 3 minutes are up Touchy can take of the blindfold and go over the results.

7 Another player is chosen as Touchy and the game resumes as before. The player with the most discoveries wins.

IMPORTANT MESSAGE

KEEP ON SWIMMING ! NO MATTER WHAT, JUST

AN OBVIOUS ANSWER?

I AM NOT ALIVE, BUT I GROW; I DON'T HAVE LUNGS,
BUT I NEED AIR. I DON'T HAVE A MOUTH,
BUT WATER KILLS ME. WHAT AM I?

WHO'S THIS?

WHALE, FISH, SQUID

THIS IS THE CLASSIC GAME OF ROCK, PAPER, SCISSORS CONVERTED INTO HILARIOUS, ACTING FUN!

1 Setup

Players can range from 2 to 10. The group is split into two teams.

2

Split the room or outdoor field into 3 parts. Two safe parts for each team and one battlefield in the middle. The teams go to their safe parts.

3

The game is a variation of Rock, Paper, Scissors, with Whale, Fish, Squid instead. The teams have to act out the characters as follows:
WHALE: Raise your arms and chest up high and yell out loud in whalespeak (just like Dory does).
FISH: Stick out your head, suck in your chins, pout your lips and cross your eyes.
SQUID: Wiggle your arms out from your sides.

4 Play the game

The teams decide which character they will play. A neutral referee instructs the teams to go to the line of the battlefield. Everyone is ready. The referee yells 3, 2, 1 GO! and the teams jump into the battlefield playing their character.

5

The winning players now try to grab the losers, who try to get back to their safe place. The players caught are now part of the opposing team.

6

The teams huddle together and decide again which character to act. The game is over when one team is left.

7 Who beats who?

WHALE beats FISH (because it can eat them)
FISH beats SQUID (because it can outswim them)
SQUID beats WHALE (because it can squeeze them)

WHAT'S WITH THE REBUS?

YOU MAY BE FLUENT IN WHALE-SPEAK BUT CAN YOU UNDERSTAND THESE PHRASES?

FAREDCE

FUZZ
NOTHING

PPOD

LOV

T_RN

SAILING
C C C C C C

WHAT AM I?

WITH NO WINGS, I FLY.
WITH NO EYES, I SEE.
WITH NO ARMS, I CLIMB.
MORE FRIGHTENING THAN
ANY BEAST,
STRONGER THAN ANY FOE.
I AM CUNNING, RUTHLESS,
AND TALL;
IN THE END, I RULE ALL.

OCTOPUS

Hank is an octopus. They inhabit diverse regions of the ocean, including coral reefs. The octopus is considered to be the most intelligent non-vertibrate animal in the sea. They live on all kinds of shell creatures and exude black ink for camouflage and defense.

TIME OUT !

QUICK THINKING, GOOD REFLEXES AND A BIT OF LUCK DECIDE WHETHER YOUR TIME IS OUT!

1 Form 5-10 sets of questions that have multiple answers.
For instance:
What floats on water?
Name a species of fish.
Name a sea mammal. What can fly in the air?
What is hotter than air?
Name a species of whale.
... and so on.

2 A group of players sit in a circle and one, designated a Gamemaster, sits in the middle and holds all the questions. By random he/she asks a player a question, say "What floats on water?" The player has about 5 seconds to reply. Then the player to the left has to reply within the same short timeframe.

3 This goes on until a player is out of time and can't come up with an answer. He/she gets one point and the Game-master asks the player next in line a new question.

4 The player with the least points wins.

THAT WAS FUN!

AQUATIC BRAIN BOOSTERS 4

AND FINALLY SOME SILLY RIDDLES WITH A BIT OF LOGIC!

1

QUESTION:
Why did the cantaloupe jump into the ocean?

2

QUESTION:
Why do fish live in salt water?

3

QUESTION:
What do you get when you cross an elephant with a fish?

4

QUESTION:
What is the difference between a fish and a piano?

5

QUESTION:
What makes an octopus laugh?

ANSWERS

PAGE 5

AQUATIC BRAIN BOOSTERS 1
1. A memory
2. Advice
3. The young one's mother
4. Nine

PAGE 8

HOW MANY MAMMALS?
Answer: 1

PAGE 9

WHAT'S NOT RIGHT?
Answer: The otter in picture number two does not live in the sea.

WHO'S THIS?
Answer: Dory

PAGE 10

A QUESTION OF DIFFERENCE
Answer: 8

PAGE 11

THE PUZZLING WORD
Answer: Remember

AN OBVIOUS ANSWER?
Answer:
The letters above sea level have no curves. The letters under sea level all have curves.

AQUANAGRAM
Answer: Keep on swimming.

PAGE 13

TURN MARLIN AROUND

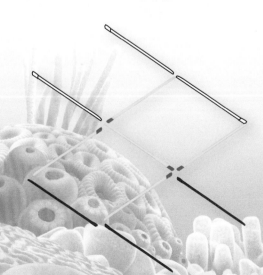

PAGE 15

WHAT'S WITH THE REBUS?
Answers:
Too funny for words
I'm shorter than you
One in a million
Forgive and forget

AN OBVIOUS ANSWER?
Answer: Phillip

PAGE 17

AQUATIC BRAIN BOOSTERS 2
1. Non-vertibrae
2. Short
3. The letter N
4. Wholesome
5. Second. If anyone crosses the second position, he/she would be in the second place because there is someone who occupied the first position.

PAGE 19

WHAT'S WITH DORY?
Answer: The first picture is the correct one.

AQUANAGRAMS
Answers:
Octopus
Shark
Whale
Parents
Memory

PAGE 21

CLOSE UP CHARACTERS
Answers:
Dory
Destiny
Nemo
Hank
Bailey

BREAK THE CODE!
Answer: Don't give up!

PAGE 23

A DIFFERENT DESTINY
Answer: Three.

LAND OR SEA
Answers:
Walk-Swim
Dry-Wet
Trees-Kelp

Hot-Cold
Tiger-Shark
Mammal-Fish
Elephant-Whale
Air-Water

PAGE 25

GEOMETRIC QUIZ
Answer: 10 times. Try drawing lines from the dots to each other. There is also a mathematical solution to this question.
Ask you teacher about it!

AN OBVIOUS ANSWER
Answer: You can't take a picture with a yellow fin!

AQUANAGRAMS
Answers:
Coral Reef	Aquarium
Ship	Submarine
Diver	Ocean

PAGE 27

THE EYES HAVE IT!
Answers:
Hank
Destiny
Dory
Bailey
Nemo

WHAT IS THIS?
Answer: Ship

PAGE 29

AQUATIC BRAIN BOOSTERS 3
1. Half way. Beyond that he is swimming out of the coral reef.
2. Pride
3. Stop imagining!
4. February. It´s the shortest month!
5. Six, since no one is there to remove the 3 dead fish.

PAGE 31

LET'S FREE NEMO!

WHAT IS THE LAW?
Answer: All words describing anything in the Archipelago must have sh in them.

PAGE 33

IMPORTANT MESSAGE
Answer:
You are fabulous, just the way you are.

AN OBVIOUS ANSWER?
Answer: Silence.

WHAT'S GOING TO HAPPEN?
Answer: I'll be back!

PAGE 35

PALINDROMES
Answers:
SOS
Kayak
Eye
Abba

WHAT AM I?
Answer: The letter e.

PAGE 37

LET'S FREE NEMO ... AGAIN!

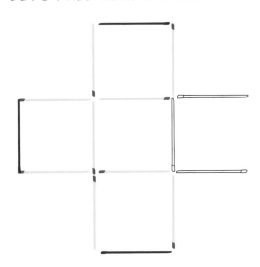

AQUANAGRAMS
Answers:
Ancor
Rope
Sailor
Captain

WHAT AM I?
Answer: A fish!

PAGE 39

IMPORTANT MESSAGE
Answer:
No matter what, just keep on swimming!

AN OBVIOUS ANSWER?
Answer: Fire

WHO'S THIS?
Answer: Destiny. Des+tincan-can+y.

PAGE 41

WHAT'S WITH THE REBUS?
Answers:
Red in the face
Big fuzz over nothing
Two peas in a pod
Endless love
No U turn
Sailing the seven seas

WHAT AM I?
Answer: Imagination!

PAGE 43

AQUATIC BRAIN BOOSTERS 4
1. Because it wanted to be a watermellon!
2. Because pepper makes them sneeze!
3. Swimming trunks
4. You can tune a piano but you can´t tuna fish!
5. Tentacles (ten tickles).